"Quick, effective marketing, motivational & mystical messages driving you to success"

The Money Is In Serving Others, Not In Helping Others

Vol. 28 In The *Sub 4 Minute Extra Mile* Series

by

Ted Ciuba, Ph.D.

The Money Is In Serving Others, Not In Helping Others

Vol. 28 In The *Sub 4 Minute Extra Mile* Series

ISBN: 978-1493753284

by **Ted Ciuba**

© MMXIIII PTIPTrust, *all rights reserved*

www.ThinkRich.com

info@thinkrich.com

Parthenon Marketing Inc
2400 Crestmoor Rd #36
Nashville TN 37215   USA

Orders & Enrollments

+1-877- *4 RICHES*

***

phone +1-615-662-3169

"Who Else Wants Quantum Coach and Author Ted Ciuba To Stimulate A Quantum Leap In Your Group?"

Schedule permitting, Dr. Ted Ciuba welcomes keynote, speaking and training invitations from businesses, churches, organizations, associations, & promoters.

Combines the spiritual purpose of quantum consciousness as per *The John Gospel Code* with the quantum performance message of *The New Think And Grow Rich, 101 Quantum Success Secrets,* and *Sub 4 Minute Extra Mile.*

For anyone in wholesome pursuit of money, a career, sales, indeed, achievement of any kind, as well as a life and service.

Through a brief, relevant pre-event questionnaire, presentation is made unique to each group.

To start conversation:

www.ThinkRich.com/invite

+1-615-662-3169

Ted Ciuba On Stage In LA

Defy & Re-Define The Status Quo In Short, Regular, Focused, Intense, Intended Training Sessions

www.BigBriefMoments.com

Complete your collection! Give a meaningful gift!

The *Sub 4 Minute Extra Mile* Series

High impact training focused on human potential, marketing, & that holomagic c^2 factor

To get ahead you've got to go the *extra mile*

Redefine personal & professional possibility!

A sampling of what you'll find…

Vol: Title

001: Create Your Life By Design

002: Know Your Purpose, Embrace Adventure

003: That HoloMagic c2 Factor

004: A Single Reason Why

005: Same Winds, Different Direction

006: The Day Superman Died

And many more!

http://BigBriefMoments.com

www.BigBriefMoments.com

"Amazing New Audio Program Gives You Both The Magic Formula To Riches & Most Effective Technology To Make It Happen Quickly And Easily!"

<u>Audio Version</u> of…

The New Think and Grow Rich
Quantum Version

by Ted Ciuba

Read by the Author!

Get the full story at...

This goes way BEYOND the amazing material captured in the book, *The NEW Think and Grow* by Ted Ciuba, into...

Learning Styles

All the "content" in the world, put in book form just doesn't make the connection with most people...

It's just a fact, most people find reading too much a struggle to put up with...

Some people find it impossible to get the meaning from squiggles on a page...

"I read the book years and years ago, but I didn't get the depth of it till I heard you narrating it."

Vita Buffa

101 Quantum Success Secrets

Author Ted Ciuba put these quantum secrets together and makes them freely available to you. **$197 value, *FREE!***

101 Success Secrets
101 Training Sessions
101 Seconds Each

Turn your life around.
 Stay focused.
  Achieve your dreams.

www.ThinkRich.com/101successsecrets

 Think Rich Ministries

Donate To Think Rich Ministries

It does take money to spread the Word throughout this material world. All donations are appreciated and are invested to spread Quantum Humanism.

www.ThinkRich.com/donate

 Think Rich Radio

www.ThinkRichRadio.com

"Voice Of Quantum Humanism"

Relevant conversations for today.

"Discover The "Secret" In A Magical Mastermind Study Of The 1937 *Original Publication* Of Napoleon Hill's Success Classic, *Think And Grow Rich!*"

Achiever's MasterMind

Achiever's MasterMind

You actively participate in working study sessions...

Designed With The Sole Purpose Of Making You Wealthy!

www.AchieversMasterMind.com

Includes:

1. Sixteen Achiever's MasterMind Sessions In Audio
2. Achiever's MasterMind Study Chapters
3. *Achiever's MasterMind* Study Guides

Bonuses include word-for-word transcriptions!

- How to do direct imprinting into your nervous system, so that you're driven to success!

- How to harness the awesome unseen power that has created Fortunes with one secret 6-step technique. (Takes less than 5 minutes to implement.)

- The 8-part, no-fail secret the winners in the wealth game use to... Create your own "breaks"

- And much, much more!

www.AchieversMasterMind.com

"If You're Looking For That Decided Edge That Can Accelerate You To Riches!…"

Author of *The NEW Think And Grow Rich*, Ted Ciuba, journeyed East to forge this collaboration. The entire event was captured, & is available to you now as the…

East-West Success MasterMind
www.EastWestSuccessMasterMind.com

Share the excitement that got people tuning in from Singapore, Malaysia, China, Hong Kong, Vietnam, Korea, Philippines, Thailand, India, Australia, UK, USA, Africa, and Latin America!

The purpose of the MasterMind is quite simple...

In a MasterMind study of the success philosophy outlined in the original *Think And Grow Rich*…

- ➤ To merge the BEST of both East and West to enable any willing human being, anywhere on this planet *or any other planet or moon*, to THINK WITH INTENT…

- ➤ To control and direct your thinking to receive the *natural result* of RICHES in your life!

"One of the most important days of my life was the day I began to read Think and Grow Rich." - W. Clement Stone

"I was invited to participate in the MasterMind *study of* Think And Grow Rich *by my friend Ted Ciuba. That 8-week program transformed my own Consciousness of Wealth...* - Dan Klatt

www.EastWestSuccessMasterMind.com

Finally Discovered!
Bible Secrets Hidden 1,917 Years Laid Bare

The John Gospel CODE
Unveiling The Contraband Message
by Ted Ciuba

To sum up John's problem and his charge…

➤ John is the only person on Earth
  in possession of the illumined
  words Jesus spoke to his
  initiatic inner circle
  that **fateful final evening**…

John wanted to effectively transmit
the **mystic message** of Jesus to a
future epoch of humanity through a
present **age of mistrust and
intrigue**…

He did what he was inspired to do.
He coded it into his mysterious story
about the Christ, which became the
anchor gospel of the Biblical canon,
awaiting the magic day it could
breathe again.

The *Original* Message Unveiled!

Today we find ourselves with the code – given us in recent
years by quantum physics – which allows us to unveil the
contraband message John coded into his ununderstandable but
politically correct words.

It tells a different, far more glorious story than you've been led
to believe.

www.TheJohnGospelCode.com

> In bluntest contradiction to the mis-guided thesis
>   the Bible condemns psychic skills...

"The Bible promises psychic sensitivities as a natural concomitant to the spiritual life!"

Samuel is psychic, David keeps Gad on retainer as a psychic, Ezekiel is psychic, Peter is psychic.

The Bible, *Genesis* through *Revelation*, is **revealed through channeling**, after all.

Book reveals the **psychic dimension** is the very channel established and used by God to communicate with humanity.

> The stories of the Bible speak with mythic significance

The boundaries of the material world do not confine Spirit and Soul

> The setting is the ancient Middle East,
>   The location is everywhere; the time is always

Psi and its marvels interest everyone...

> On the other hand, **psi ability** calls its own...
> Some special individuals among us are awakening now

Psychic And Paranormal Phenomena In The Bible leads you in **develop**ing **your own psychic sensitivities** today.

Recommended Business Resources

ThinkRich.com/business

 www.AutoPilotRiches.com

The net's premier **integrated ecommerce solution**.

Includes unlimited products, unlimited database, unlimited autoresponders. Compatible with all merchant accounts, PayPal, etc

 www.FastCashDomains.com

The net's leading domain supplier. Easy management.

www.GatorWebsiteHosting.com

Unlimited Web Hosting! Unlimited disk space. Unlimited bandwidth! Easy, Affordable.

24/7/365 technical support

How To Get Rich On The Internet

www.HowToGetRichOnTheInternet.com

Mail Order In The Internet Age

www.MailOrderInTheInternetAge.com

Vol. 28 In *The Sub 4 Minute Extra Mile* Series

The Money Is In Serving Others, Not In Helping Others

by

Ted Ciuba, Ph.D.

TABLE OF CONTENTS

Introduction: It Takes So Little To Excel

As an achiever, would you agree with me that you must go the extra mile? *I thought so...*

Surely you know if you do what average people do, you'll get the same kind of average results they do. And you want more!

And it's actually quite easy to stand out, because most people wouldn't dream of going the extra mile. But for you and me, while, yes, it takes something extra, yes, it takes drive and discipline.... The amazing thing is, it takes so *little* to excel!

Roger Bannister
Runs Sub 4 Minute Mile

After all, it's called the extra *mile*, not the extra *100 miles!*

Be that as it may, we're talking about the positive rewards that come to you in any economy by going the extra mile.

It was Roger Bannister who defied and redefined history by running the sub 4 minute mile.

And the amazing thing is that Bannister did NOT spend the countless hours and hours practicing that conventional training would guide him to. He gave it what he could... In his busy pre-med Oxford schedule he took a mere 30 minutes out of his daily lunch hour to train and run. And with that he set a world record that had towered 3,000 years!

He ushered in a new era of possibility. Though no one had *ever* broken it, within 2 1/2 years time of Bannister's record-breaking, seemingly unachievable sub 4 minute mile, 18 others were doing it.

And how did he do it?... It wasn't a function of *time*.

It was *intention*. Roger Bannister, in the short, focused, regular, intense, intended few minutes per day he wrested from his busy Oxford pre-med studies was throwing himself into the sport. He gave it everything he could, as an additional interest and pursuit in his life...

You see, when Roger Bannister suffered the ignominious defeat of coming in 5th place in the 1952 Olympics, right then and there, he determined to be the first human to run the sub 4 minute mile!

It was just a "thought". It's just another instance and undisputable illustration, my friend, of the power of intention powered by determination.

Moments before 6 pm on 6 May 1954, he takes a breath of vision and determination. He feels it! He confides to his pacemakers "The sub 4 minute attempt is on!"

Short moments later the shot is fired... The runners are off!! Roger Bannister breaks the string at the end of the mile in 3 minutes, 59 seconds, and 4/10's, trailblazing into the sub 4 minute mile age!

Recognition Point!! - This was NOT an unintended event! Recognition point!! Little efforts, little accomplishments - short, focused, regular, intense, intended training sessions - gear into colossal events!

This didn't happen by good luck or timing... Roger Bannister didn't "drift" over the finish line into the annals of history... It was the thing he geared all his intentions to accomplish, even though he didn't spend hours and hours a day in the quest to achieve it.

Which names this series, The *Sub 4 Minute Extra Mile*...

➢ Now you, honoring Roger Bannister's history-setting accomplishments and methods, can make the same kind of history-breaking progress in sub 4 minutes a day!
➢ Now you can defy your own status quo in short, focused, regular, intense, intended training sessions and redefine your personal possibilities!

And Then It Looks Like You Were Lucky

We all like to get lucky. But you can't depend on luck and good fortune in building your career. Luck is just the cards of a single day; it's just something that happens.

And even then, if you're not playing the right game with the right players at the right time, how much benefit will you get from those four aces you drew? It's not just luck the people who get ahead experience. Nooo. The luck that *they* have is the luck they sowed over time with their organized planning, effort, and diligence. The luck they have is a result of the work and effort they've invested already.

Arnold Schwarzenegger did not become Mr. Universe by luck. Nor did he become an actor by good fortune, just because he was Mr. Universe. Nor did he become Governor of California by luck.

No, those who believe in luck are really taking the long and torturous way... It's funny how they persist in their illusions. Any observer can see they're taking the long road to *failure*, but they can't see it.

Even if some incredible luck should strike, the very nature of luck does not lend itself to building a career. It's not a trend, it's just an event.

Sometimes the stars do align propitiously, and you find yourself involved in something that is genuinely "lucky," as, for instance, you could have been living through the de-regulation of AT&T, the telephone giant, if you live in the U.S. All of a sudden, lots of opportunities sprang up for several different companies, and millions were made quickly.

Yet those who profited were those who happened to be standing nearby, already involved in that business when the explosion fired! They had to seize it and squeeze it immediately for all it was worth.

Millions were made by several people. But despite those millions, it was only by good fortune they could jump into the newly de-regulated opportunity and *work*. That's the four-letter word that causes most people to miss the gravy train of life, by the way, *w-o-r-k*.

And there's another opportunity on top of you right now. As I speak they are in the process of de-regulating household energy, such as gas, coal, and electricity. There are a lot of opportunities, and there are several companies out there taking advantage of them. But their luck consists of more than just good accidental timing… They're working very hard to capitalize on the opening luck has gifted them, alongside worthy competitors snapping at their piece of the pie.

Luck is an event.

Are you truly ready for a stroke of good luck? Only then can you make anything of it.

Fortune is created by persistent, intelligent, directed effort. And then it *looks* like you were lucky.

It's How We Live and How We Love In The Present

My dear friend lost her husband recently... It must have been peaceful for him. He was still in his morning lotus position when they found him. But for her? All of her dreams, ambitions, and activities had been centered around and connected with that man no longer here.

As an observer of humankind, I can affirm, if there ever was "a match made in Heaven," this was the one.

You bet it's got to be a game changer. It amazes me how rapidly a curve-ball like this can come at us.

This is not the first one for her, either. She lost a daughter, 23 years old, who just was sick, but the pharmacy erred and gave her one hundred times the dose.

Game changers, both of them. Now, of course, she needs a few days to grieve. Let's give her that grace. Radical change swoops in on eagles' wings.

I feel for her because of the suddenness and gravity of it. On the other hand, she's still a young enough woman to bounce back - and she will. Two or three years from now, she could even have another spouse, or a business helping new widows through the transition.

But I know those weren't just stories of their fairytale romance, because I was there. I admired the chivalric respect he treated her with. And I'm certain it can't be easy to find a replacement for that guy.

And while I participate in her grieving, I also know she will get on with her life. Because there is no other option.

In the final analysis, all of us, as human beings, if we do good, celebrate living the good time we have, and then we disappear.

Everything in her life was connected to, with, and around this noble man. But there is no security in life. And her having her life connected with him is the way it *should* be, even in the midst of insecurity. Love is the only commandment.

Living the adventure of life is not about cowering under what *may* happen in the future, though we know it may... We'll always adjust. It's how we live and how we love in the *present.*

He left. She's still got more celebrating to do, and she certainly treats this time now as the *present* it is.

Passionate, Engaging Adventure Or Painful Grey Conformity?

It has been said by numerous philosophers, including Viktor Frankl in *Man's Search For Meaning,* written in the WWII German concentration camps about the experience there, that the one thing that we have that can't be taken away is the ability to choose our thoughts.

That is, we can be forced into the most atrocious bodily servitude, yet we always retain the ability to keep our mind focused on what we want.

That gives us incredible power to bring richness into any circumstance. You do know you'll have setbacks, right? Yes, of course. Will you have issues with your spouse, or kids, or parents? Yes, of course. Will you dent the car? Yes, of course. Will you experience setbacks in business, like maybe a promotion you coveted and didn't get? Yes, of course.

All that. But so does everybody else; it's part and parcel of life. So that's not the real issue. The issue is, you *will* pass time. In this dimension you're in a linear passage through your lifespan.

So the question is, will you make your one go-round journey a passionate, engaging adventure, or a painful grey conformity?

The human animal *does* have free will. The human animal can control its thoughts, and create its experience. It can take setbacks, like many athletes have done, and turn them into the very stuff of their next achievement. Or they can wimper into insignificance thinking they're not good enough, not sweet enough, not tall enough, not short enough, not young enough, not old enough, not green enough, and not white enough, either. It's up to you. The debilitating particulars are filled in by each individual's unconscious.

Are you going for passionate, engaging adventure or sliding toward a painful grey conformity? Will you create a life of joy and passion, or is yours to suffer pain?

You only get one experience, no matter what that one is. You can choose to assert your human dominion and actualize in the worst of circumstances, like Sir Edmund Hillary, who began writing his book, *The Scottish Himalayan Expedition,* on the only paper he had - toilet paper. And the Gestapo found it, and destroyed it.

And he began again. Eventually he got that book published. It was important to him to write because he didn't think he'd ever be able to climb again, decimated as he was by the experience of being in a concentration camp, undernourished and in ill health. He chose to use his inner powers in ways he could in the circumstances he was in. And we're still quoting him today.

It's your choice, just like it was Edmund Hillary's. What are you doing with *your* life?

The Payoff Of Knowledge Versus The Penalty Of Its Lack

I recently saw a fat man running down the street, his flabby breasts and belly flopping around. This is not the first time I've seen him, so we've got to give him points for that. I would suggest a different place than the street, but that's a whole nother story. What *is* the story here is that he's doing what he needs to do... He thinks.

But he doesn't have the insight to be effective. It's a fatal flaw. He doesn't know that unless he also regulates his diet, he can run and suffer all he wants, but he's never going to lose the weight he's working to lose. Neither diet nor physical activity work in isolation. Together they create synergy.

Too many people do the physical activity - the exercise - and never give thought to diet. Part of that reason is they believe, through mis-education at school, mirrored in society, they get an adequately healthy diet. They don't.

The long and the short of it is, when they go out to run they think they're doing the right thing. In truth they're not doing half the right thing, not half right.

If this person would simply start eating an alkaline diet, he would find himself losing weight without all this work.

Bad diet equals bad results.

Good diet equals good results.

One doesn't have to be either a math whiz or a dietician to recognize what's happening.

In other words, here's how difficult it is... Eat fresh fruits and vegetables, nuts, and grains. No more. No meats, poultry, fish, or dairy.

You can be as stupid as I am and trim down like I have. You know me as a trim person. Yet I once lost three belt sizes and 35 pounds in 70 days, and it all has to do with shifting from what I thought was a decent diet to what I now know to be a far better diet.

I had to give the *"¡Adios!"* to my entire wardrobe! Only the shoes survived the weight loss...

The system programs us with errors. Some say they do it intentionally.

I can tell you two things:

1. Deeper knowledge is available for the inquiring spirit
2. You can clearly see the payoff of knowledge versus penalty of its lack

Why don't you give the vegan raw food diet a chance and see what it does for you? Experience how much better it makes you feel. Trying to substitute book knowledge for living experience with a good diet could best be compared to imagining what it's like to swim in a stormy sea versus being in the stormy sea swimming.

You can always slide back to your sloppy diet if you don't quickly start trimming down, feeling younger, and bristling with energy.

For Both Shakespeare And Your Mom

Shakespeare says it…

"Oftentimes excusing of a fault doth make the fault the worse by
the excuse."

Did your mother ever say to you?..

"It was bad enough that you did it, don't make it worse by lying
about it."

Nobody likes an excuse maker. Who wants to hear what they
already know you're guilty of? Who wants to hear excuses when
they were expecting results?

A significant part of becoming a contributor, actualized, and
stepping up to fulfill the leadership role is taking responsibility.
That's outside of and in addition to the career specific specialized
knowledge one would presumably have.

It's the losers who make excuses.

Sure, we're all human, and everybody's done it at some time,
but it's like anything else. Once you "catch yourself" doing it, you
can change your behavior. Awareness comes first. Commitment
comes to the conscious. You can take responsibility.

Something like this might do the trick:

"I accept responsibility. What I did was wrong, and I want to make
it right."

That's how simple it can be. As a bonus, you're practicing culture at the same time. You'll feel far better.

Once you knew your behavior was hurting or threatening another, you wouldn't continue your irresponsible behavior, so don't make something worse by failing to admit to your faults. Be grateful someone pointed them out.

I'm sure, since it's important enough for both Shakespeare and your mom to remind you, it's something you want to seriously consider.

Our Doubts Are Traitors

I'm a Shakespeare freak, what can I say? His work is popular even in Latin America, where I spend a lot of my time. His name is so famous they don't translate it; they say it in Spanish exactly as it's said in English. His wisdom is universal; it doesn't apply only if you're in the Northern Hemisphere, above the equatorial line. It applies throughout human culture and history.

One of the things Shakespeare teaches us is:

"Our doubts are traitors, and make us lose the good we oft might win, by fearing to attempt."

From the greatest motivators to the man who understood all of human nature, the message is the same... You've got to have faith. You've got to believe you can do it before you can do it. You've got to be willing to go out there and put yourself on the line.

Until you get that white hot passion of belief vested in knowing you *will* have what you're going for, you're your own biggest enemy.

Feel the reality of your dreams. Buy into the vision of your dreams as your genuine *conditional* tomorrow... Conditioned only upon your approach. You've got to believe you can do it before you can do it.

But There's A Millionaire Reasons Why

I hear all kinds of excuses from people telling me why they can't do something I have every reason to expect a normally functioning adult in today's society should do. And I'm talking about people who say they want to get ahead!

I ran across one lady arguing for her incapacity around electronics. Seems like a good excuse to visit the bone yard while you're still breathing.

When it comes right down to it, you can offer them all the free training you want, but you can't make them *do* anything with it. It's like putting a plate of health-enhancing food in front of them and they brush it aside asking for double hamburgers and salty fries.

I don't spend much time listening to people who aren't serious enough to take action, and I won't give them the shine-on they're looking for, either, because it's too easy to do. There's no reason why you can't listen to your iPod when you're doing your chores or going to work. There's no reason why you can't get an iPod that plays videos. There's no *reason* why you can't take written material with you on a notebook.

Oh, this is a good one, and I hear it all the time: "I don't like e-books because I have to print them off." Well, no, you don't. But even if you did, very good laser printers are affordable today. Paper is affordable. Of course, you could learn to read on screen, the way people do in the new millennium.

There's no reason why you *can't* sort your affairs and grow into technology. But there's a millionaire reasons why you should.

Napoleon Hill's Gratitude Prayer – More Than You Think

People speak of Napoleon Hill's "Gratitude Prayer" as if "it" was the only one. Actually, there's two versions he left us, which is not surprising for a dignitary often asked to bless the table at events he attended.

Here we share those two different versions of his "Gratitude Prayer." The first version really is more of a petition, but it's circulating as a gratitude prayer.

If you already know Napoleon Hill, you'll see him in the words. If you don't know him yet, these are quintessential statements revealing the man...

Here's the first prayer famous under his name:

> "Oh Divine Providence, I ask not for more riches, but for more wisdom to make wiser use of the riches you gave me at birth, consisting in the power to direct my own mind to whatever ends I desire."

That's what I call the holomagic prayer. It helps us understand where the corpus of power is: in Divine Providence, in HoloCosm.

You don't have to ask for more riches if you ask for more wisdom to use the riches you've been given. That's the indisputable logic of the Napoleon mind, and it's truly so wise, how could anyone argue against it?

Here is the wisdom and power, precisely in your discrimination to which ends you direct your mind. That could be getting rich, it could be funding 180 missionaries for your faith, it could be anything - *whatever ends* you desire.

Powerful! And here's the second version of his gratitude prayer, the one more clearly expressing *gratitude*. The wording is only slightly different, because he ends up speaking of the same faith in the creative power of the human mind…

> "I give thanks daily, not for mere riches, but for the wisdom with which to recognize, embrace, and properly use the great abundance of riches I now have at my command."

That "great abundance of riches" he refers to, is none other than that "power to direct my own mind to whatever ends I desire."

There you have it: the two circulating versions of Napoleon Hill's "Gratitude Prayer."

And take it on my word, you'll find a certain delight everytime someone speaks of Napoleon Hill's Gratitude Prayer as if it's the only one, and you get to enter the conversation with enlightenment on a very beneficial topic.

Let us give thanks Napoleon Hill left these fine prayers for us, but more importantly, let's put them to the *use* he intended…

"Let us pray. We give thanks…."

Over That Double Rainbow

If you have a single fiber of humanity in your soul, it won't surprise you that when Carmel Maguire, wife of Frank Maguire, sang, "Somewhere Over The Rainbow" at his funeral, everybody cried.

Frank was a very successful businessman, co-founder with Fred Smith of FedEx, the idea that wouldn't work. Fred Smith couldn't get a job; Frank Maguire couldn't *hold* a job. After some conversation, they figured, "Okay, what do we have to lose? Let's start this company." And you know what happened next.

Recent years he was a motivational speaker who inspired insights and actions with positive results which will last a lifetime for thousands upon thousands… And with the Internet, print, audio, and video, his influence has not gone away.

That final day Carmel took him to the airport she saw the most *beauuuutiful* double rainbow. And they awed together…

You know how rare a double rainbow is. It's the kind of thing that, in a lifetime, may only happen twice. So she turned to Frank and said, "That's a sign today is going to be the best day *ever*!"

He agreed, kissed her bye, and got on the plane. That plane took him over that double rainbow into eternity.

♫ "Somewhere over the rainbow…" ♪ - or should that be, ♪♪♫ "Over the double rainbow…" ♪?

She sang. They cried.

People Prefer To Do Business With Those They Know, Like, And Trust

The other day I needed some video equipment. I picked up a phone, called my friend, and said, "This is what I'm trying to do; what do you recommend? Okay, send it to me."

That's all that has to happen.

This guy is not necessarily the flashiest guy in his business, or the one making the most money, but he's getting my business.

Why? Because we're friends. We have worked together, we have suffered together, we have made money together, we have laughed and cajoled together. We've been out on the lake together.

All things being equal, and even a lot of times all things *not* being equal, people prefer to do business with those they know, like, and trust.

If I were to call up someone else out of the blue… You know that uneasy feeling wondering if they're trying to get one over on you. "Can I trust them?" "Do you really care about me?"

How often have you heard that you need to network? It's *true*. That's how we met.

You need to be out there being helpful, spreading your message. Then when people discover you care about them, and they know, like, and trust you, and they know you're capable, that you have decent prices… When they have a need, you're the one. Can you ask for anything more?

This is an especially important message in this Internet Age, when people believe all they need to do to make money is sign up for a few affiliate programs, find some good keywords, put up an optimized blog, and buy some banners. And yes, you can make a living that way, but you can't make a *life* that way.

You've got to think long term. Think *relationships*. All things being equal, people always prefer someone they know, like, and trust for the business they're going to give to somebody anyway. This is true whether you're a plumber, an attorney, an accountant, an internet marketing consultant, or a roofer. Be sociable, be friendly. Let people know you exist for *them*.

Build relationships, and then you'll have an asset that can truly make you cash on demand, simply by offering them another valuable product they *want*.

Debrief Is An Integral Part Of The Success Process

You'd be amazed at how much this one little exercise can help you. Overall, it's part of being conscious, but it's something a lot of people overlook.

First, whenever you set an objective or event, you automatically set goals, criteria, and objectives. An adept in organized planning considers and sets markers, mileposts, guides – as in 'if this, then that' or 'when this, then that.' It comes in the conception. We but refine what we start out with.

A sound mind looks for clarity on certain simple, but key points before you rally and hustle out the unthinking door…

> ➤ What do I want to accomplish?
> ➤ How will I measure success?

Not complicated; but it is focused. Then you go out and do the job. Right here, however, after you've triumphed or faltered, or any point in between, comes the important step most omit… And then you *reflect*. It's called a *debrief* or an *after action review* in the organizational environment.

It's not complicated, and requires more of *consciousness* than it does of "brains," in the conventional sense. You simply answer these questions…

> ➤ How did we measure up?

➢ What did we do well?

➢ How could we perform better?

➢ What do we do different next time?

➢ What do we do now?

To optimize any process, you need to debrief. This isn't just after a military mission, like you've seen on TV, it's the same thing in a business context, and even relating to the family vacation.

First you have an idea, a goal, an objective you're aiming toward. Then you set and refine guidelines and targets, gather resources, and mobilize... Then you debrief and adjust.

The process is summarized:

1. Objective
2. Guidelines & Goals
3. Action
4. Debrief & Adjust

It repeats. The specifics are unique to the situation, the environment, and the incident, but the process of being conscious before, during, and *after* the event is how you make progress among specifics...

You now have feedback you loop into the process which makes the next time progressively better in performance. It will be *better* because you took time to counsel and train from the best teacher there is, *experience*.

There's the saying: "He says he's got 20 years experience, but he doesn't. He's really got one year of experience repeated 20 times." Debrief and application make the difference.

You, on the other hand, are building something with the work you do, not just passing time... You make consistent progress achieving your goals because they are meaningful enough to you that you approach the *entire* process with consciousness and follow through.

Anybody can do the thrilling stuff of setting challenging, desirable objectives. That's fun. But few will groom themselves and their actions to make it manifest. That's work.

Debrief and adjustment is an integral part of the success process. It's so integral, success cannot happen without it.

Work For Yourself

Most people miss it with the most fundamental issue we humans must resolve, work.

You could say, "I work for Bell South," or "I work for Delta Airlines." But today let's go a little deeper…

Who do you *really* work for?

Why, of course, you work for *yourself*, not for Delta or Bell South, or you name who.

They've got a "job" for you. Sure, in a very real sense, you're working for them. Yet consider that you have YOUR life to live, and, in reality, you are trading portions of that precious life you're loaned for money.

It's only familiarity with the process that keeps you from recognizing it for what it is.

Consider a similar situation… You're on a train. The train is going somewhere and you can be seated or you can even walk around *inside* the car, but you're still on someone else's train going to someone else's destination.

Now, if that train coincides with where you want to go, if it's taking you where your personal ambitions are, then this is a good thing. If not, you should reconsider.

Open the confessional to honest examination to the train of thought manifest in these questions:

> ➢ With the few years of life I have in my hands, am I achieving things that will make a difference?

> ➢ Am I achieving things that will care for me in my golden years?

> ➢ Am I achieving things that will make my children, my grandchildren, my society, my country, my planet and this universe better off?

> ➢ Or am I wasting my precious moments of opportunity working for someone else?

And I'm not saying Bell Helicopter or Delta Airlines isn't making a better world, or anybody else. Certainly those two organizations provide needed services to humanity as we know it now. But if you're inside an organization, you are selling your services to them.

You're still working for yourself, as in you have other options. It's just that you're choosing to fit into the mold they've designed for you. And you do that willingly selling yourself for a paycheck.

You may not be getting the most out of your working life as you can. Because you also are selling your viewpoint, your time, your effort, opinions, loyalty, and opportunity cost – all the other things you could be doing with the time – on a train going to a destination of someone else's choosing.

It may not be important to you, and you may feel you're getting enough out of your job. If that's you, you're a rare bird! But you can work for yourself knowledgeably and consciously, and make a difference in the world at the same time.

It's a rougher road. It starts with accepting unacceptable truths. The rewards are worth it.

You Get It, You Produce More

Why should you *embrace* outsourcing? Let me just give you one little example, to which I believe everybody can relate, and which applies equally across the board.

As I write this, I just arrived from my morning walk. I like to do that before I get in the office. Stretch the legs, aerate the lungs, breathe in rhythm, walk rapidly, think positive thoughts, and generally start to purring the imaginative programming in the body and brain...

That said, I passed the guys who are taking care of the lawn... It's 8:30, and they just drove up a few minutes ago. They're already soaked with sweat. They came from a place nearby.

They've got a giant mower, not to mention the truck and the trailer, and then they've got two weedeaters, and then they've got shovels, and rakes, and everything else.

And I think, "Ooh, man! I'm glad I pay *them* to do this."

And they also get the whole thing done very quickly. I've never timed it, but, portal to portal, it can't be much more than twenty minutes. They descend as a team with the right equipment, devour it, and back away, looking for another body, it seems...

It was a bit different the last time I tried doing the job... One day at the beginning of the season some year ago, the lawnmower wouldn't start. So I had to go to True Value Hardware to get a sparkplug. Of course, I had to find out the right kind of sparkplug first. Then I had to buy an oil can, because I wanted to squirt a little oil in the cylinder before I turned it over a few times, since it hadn't moved since the year prior… And it wouldn't start. Then I figured it couldn't breathe, so then I had to clean the air filter. I didn't have any place to do that job, and I had to go out again to buy a tray to do it in. Of course, if I was going to have gasoline, I had to locate and buy a gasoline can, and then, on the way home from that errand I stopped to buy gasoline. (Making a place to store that fuel on my property is another story…)

I finally got all the tasks done, and was ready to test out the tune up, when I discovered I didn't have anywhere to discard the dirty gasoline I had used to clean the filter with.

And *then* I had to dress differently, the way I don't, normally. I had to put on jeans, a long sleeved shirt, and goggles so I could go out in the heat, stir up the dust, and eat true grit.

Work, sweat, and struggle… I mount and fall from these murderous Tennessee hills…

And you only need to add onto the job the forty-five minutes it took me to drink a cool pop, bathe, and get back in my day…

After all was said and done, it was very expensive for me to do it myself. And it was very disruptive of my life and affairs.

Instead, I decided to pay this little company - only in season, only when they do work, and I can put them off when I want to. I have it on an every two weeks schedule because it works well, and that's about the rate the grass grows.

It's freedom. It's quick, it's effortless, and the billing is downright reasonable. They're happy to have the work; and perform it well. I'm happy to help the economy – and myself.

Now do you see why you should consider outsourcing? You get it, you produce more.

Let *them* do what they're far better at, what *they've* got the equipment, the skills, the love for, and you get on with doing your own higher leverage work.

They're finished. I did my exercises and tuned up for publication this very article, you see.

You could receive and sketch out the idea for the next *Mona Lisa* or breakthrough invention in the time you save from less productive pursuits, working where your genius lies.

The Money Is In Serving Others Not In Helping Others

You bet there's a market out there. As a matter of fact, I am one of their patrons, so I can guarantee there's a market there.

But here's my question... And it's a fundamental question related to business. When you go into business, do you go into business to serve your passion and make some income doing that? Or do you go into business primarily to make an income? There's a big difference between the two.

Because, sure, there's a market for everything, but not all markets are created equal.

Recently I went to a food court at a big mall with several members of my family. I went for the vegetarian choice, and selected and received a salad. I loved it. I sauntered straight up to the front of the counter, placed my order, and received my healthy meal. I was their market.

Meanwhile, the line that had the grilled and barbecued chicken, beef, and the like had over a hundred people in it. Now those folks had a wait time! My other family members were in that line. (So my food went uncrisp waiting the 45 minutes it took them to fight for their meal... ;)

I had a lot of free time waiting on them, and I mused to myself, "Whoa, now! As a vendor, what would you want to sell here?"

Sure, my heart and practice is in vegetarianism. Personally. Yet, it is sooo obvious that the product you would choose to sell in that mall at lunch time depends on what your objectives for the business are. It would seem to relate to the question…

> ➢ Are you in business to support a cause or to maximize your honest profits for the time and resources you invest?

You may or may not believe in the high-cholesterol, high-fat content, salty, greasy diet that's just sliding people down the road to heart problems, kidney problems, liver problems, diabetes, and you name it. We know that to be true; but what do people buy? **What do people *want* to buy?**

As a merchant, you should take up the mantle of *being* a merchant, delivering to people what they want to buy. Sure, they might be better off with a healthy diet. But the money is in serving others, not in helping others.

Don't mix your business and your passion. Hey, I've got mine, too, and I love it - on the side, please.

Bring Back Evidence From Experiences In Meditation

Whether it's self-administered or through a guided participation, meditation is an experiential passage, and its benefits can be greatly enhanced by journaling.

The reason it's hard to remember the inspired breakthroughs that come to you during meditation is that to even get there you have to forget your "self." To cross the portals between the objectified world and the psychi-spiritual realms, you must "go universal." In doing that you forget who you are, and even *that* you are. It's a lot like being in a dream state.

You can have tremendous experiences in this liminal state. Psychiatric writing as well as the literature a Virgil or a Shakespeare produces affirm the same thing: the inner world reflects the outer world; as without, so within.

> Remember, SupbraConscious is actively engaged in *wanting* to communicate with and through you...
>
> If you will only listen, interpret, and follow on.

But the problem is the messages don't always get through. They're trying... And both Sigmund Freud and Carl Jung, pioneers in serious, clinical dream work, underscore the importance of repeated dreams. Like dreams, the visions and impressions identify both the problem *and* the solution. Nothing is without purpose at this level.

Experienced travelers affirm that if you have "evidence" from the trip, evidence that you can interpret, then you may find it easier to perceive and interpret that inner communication and incorporate its counsels into your *beta* life, like you're intended to and want to do.

Such evidence might be things like drawings, plans, notes, sketches, quotes, symbols, written impressions... Evidence that exists from the time you were transported into a space too sublime to impress the human nervous system... Sacred evidences containing the keys to the mysteries of your existence.

For magic to work, you have to do your part with consciousness, too, ask any professional... If you are prepared in advance, by having your environment staged to include your favored capturing tools – such as a sketch pad and chalk, or a notepad and your digits – you can let your nervous system take down the evidence as it flows through. If you'll relax, it will come. Remember, SupbraConscious is actively engaged in *wanting* to communicate with and through you...

If you will only listen, interpret, and follow on.

Then as these impressions and images, this guidance, and mysterious whisperings arise, without breaking the liminal entrancement you're in, you journal as you choose...

Forget any grammatical or finishing considerations for the moment. Go for the broad strokes, sweep forward. You're not waking, you're staying in that holomagical *theta* brainwave state, far, so far from *beta* consciousness.

Only thing is, this time, when you wake to living in the normal world, you've got a record of your experiences. It may serve as the first thread of, or as the complete image of, the entire truth... But either way, now you've got a record. It's like coming back from another planet in your dream with a jewel, a gem, or a rock that proves when you wake you were there.

That's what journaling does for you; it gives you something you can look at, objectify, get conscious on, tune up, and incorporate into your advancing life.

A lot of times journaling serves as the one additional highly-leveraged component in your meditation regimen that real-izes the hermetic axiom, "As within; so without."

Helping Others Become Successful

The host turns to him with a mic and intros with, "Tell us what motivates you."

And the celebrity begins... "What motivates me most is helping other people gain financial independence by earning their own home-based income."

I heard a few snickers ripple through the crowd. Not everybody snickered; most people pricked up their ears. Those were the smart ones.

This man is a top earner in his company. Then he went on to say, "Yes, I *am* in a multi-level marketing company, but I will not go into those details now."

And he continued with, "But my success is keyed to and dependent on the success of those I help."

That is true. His income is dependent on his downline, on the alignment of his message with your message, the alignment of his actions with the actions that coincide with uniting and helping others become successful. That is how he becomes successful. He can't do it without you.

So believe him when he says, "My greatest desire today is to help you become super successful in your life and in your business," because it's true.

Through The Dimensions That Divide Us Now

I never told my father how much I appreciate the things that he did, like taking me fishing, getting out on Saturday morning and doing the run-around chores... Like sneaking me out when all the house was still asleep to the early morning service on Sunday. And I think of these things and more I got from Dad and the things we did together.

Now that I'm thinking about it, I really appreciate so many of the things my dad did... And I can now see the obstacles he was forced to overcome doing it. There was no such thing as layaway for expensive new toys – not with seven kids, six of them boys... Like the time it came of nature for the boys to begin exploring motors and vehicles, dad couldn't just buy one go-kart. So he found a go-kart rink that was going out of business and purchased their entire inventory of carts and spare parts!

And for several years of our youth we lived freedom and joy few could dream of...

Just a few days ago, for no real reason, I parted my hair differently, and in the comments I received, I relived Dad, well over a half a century ago, with love in front of a lighted bathroom mirror, teaching me, standing on the edge of the bathroom sink, the hard job of dividing and combing my hair...

I also think of the things that he didn't do - every person's got their own individuality. And truth be known, he and I are different, not that it makes a big difference. I'm more the philosopher type; he's more the doer type. He majored in mechanical engineering and entered the practical arts of working with things; I majored in literature, and went into the communications arts.

Sure, our interests and applications may be different. Yet it is the qualities he taught me, though I never was aware of any process going on, that make for the productive happy human existence I now live. It's the substance and the manner of living, the attention, the dedication, and the follow through that makes each person their own victor, and these things dad taught me without teaching me.

And what would a house be without love? I learned this from Dad.

And I didn't know what to say when he was dying and I had the chance… So I cried.

Leaving me no other today but…

"Dad, I love you! Thank you for the things you taught me, thank you for the time you shared, and those intangible things like love, the desire to improve, and the urges I have to do good, even if only in humble ways.

"I didn't have the awareness or capacity to say it then, so I say it now…

"Thank you for all the gifts you've so freely given me. I will do my best to share the love you've given me, to contribute to this world, and to make you proud. Through the dimensions that divide us now, your approving smile means everything to me."

Believe In HoloMagic

It all began with a song in Spanish that basically said, "I don't believe in witchcraft."

That's a song want that said...

> "I don't believe in the immaterial dimension. I don't believe that we can affect the outcome of reality by our desires, intentions, vivid visualizations, and enactments. I don't believe we are co-creators in creation our own realities, and I don't believe we receive assistance from any supposed immaterial dimensions."

I kindly offer a different point of view. In general and in specific ways, our thoughts and words create our reality.

In the same way, not believing in the immaterial realm, the realm of holomagic, in the realm of Infinite Intelligence, in the realm quantum science has proven exists... doesn't make it untrue, it just places it inaccessible by *you*.

Whether you believe in it or not, that it exists is a *fact*. Scientists have proven this. Mystics, by the way, beat them to the punch by about 25,000 years. It's food for thought. *Not believing in something does not make it untrue.* The more correct approach is to examine closely the ideas and consider what the evidence itself shows. It's all there for you.

When you believe, when you strive and you *know* it's yours you trigger holomagic. And it happens better and before you could design things yourself...

One could say, "You applied for the job so you got the job. What's magic about that?"

Huh?

I guess it was just coincidence you weren't even looking for work. You were waiting for an airport shuttle, and there was a forgotten piece of newspaper beside you with a circled ad. You looked at it, liked it, and called the ad. *That* is holomagic, an instance when the deeper reality underlying all appearances puts in an appearance.

For my part, mark me down, and I hope you're in the same camp... You better believe I believe in holomagic!

Oh that we recognize it!

We Live, We Fly, We Die

My disclaimer in advance here is that I don't want to do this little thing, but I can't help doing it. Otherwise I strive always to be a gentleman.

However, there are certain places where I have bold boundaries. We're all like this in some department(s)... "Some more than others," the lament goes... ☺

And I share... There's a bold boundary posted by the door of my office, on not *one* but on *two* signs, both of them bilingual English-Spanish, one on both sides of the door. On the right there's on a red sign with big white lettering on it, and on the left the coloring is construction yellow and black, with identically the same message.

In the two languages on both signs it says:

Bugs Stay Outside

And live peacefully

Bichos Quedensen Afuera

Y tranquilizense

And I've also done my part, by putting up a screen... It's not perfect, but it's as good as they had on *MASH*. Still some bugs somehow sneak inside. And when they do, I'm not going to coax them out, living and free, so that they can fly on to another house.

They're already living and free. I'm going to *smash* 'em and get on with life. That's the way it is.

Outside I zig and zag with them; inside it's *zero tolerance*. I've transmitted that to them. It's a clean environment. When one invades, they have not been *conscious*, shall we say? It's a costly stupidity.

When it's summertime, I like to write with my door open. Yet those pesky jungle buggies find their way inside. In the last three days, I must have been forced to dispatch eight of 'em. Makes one wonder what the lesson might be...

This youthful bug comes exploring in, and – *Boom!* he never goes back home. Family and community simply never hear about him again; he's just MIA in life.

Same thing with those other bugs flying in the no fly zone. It sure appears that life runs until it ends.

Bug lives. Bug flies in. Bug's life ends.

Is it any different for me or for you? We could any of us go out in our car, a plane, a boat, or any other means, and never return as easily. It could happen walking to the corner store. It doesn't even take stepping outside the house to die: Elvis, *"The King is dead! Long live the King!"* died alone in his bathroom.

It surely is a message conferring urgency and the need to love *today*.

We live, we fly, we die.

THE END

About The Author

Rev. Ted Ciuba, Ph.D.

Ted Ciuba

World's Foremost Quantum Achievement Trainer
Minister-At-Large
Author

Ted Ciuba is...

World's Foremost Quantum Achievement Trainer

> Author of startling *John Gospel Code: The Contraband Message Unveiled*
> Author of bestselling *The New Think And Grow Rich*, Quantum Version, modernization of Napoleon Hill's success classic
> Original founder of World Internet Summit, largest and longest running

entrepreneurial internet marketing training organization in the world

➤ Founder of HoloCosm Ministries
➤ Coach and lead therapist of *Quantum Leap Mind Training*
➤ Author of over 500 marketing and quantum achievement articles posted on Internet
➤ Author of over 40 books on professional & personal quantum achievement, including *101 Quantum Success Secrets* and the *Sub 4 Minute Extra Mile* series

Find out more at http://ThinkRich.com

Ted Ciuba, identified as the "Napoleon Hill of the Modern Age" by *Mentors Magazine*, features a unique interdisciplinary approach that includes marketing, achievement, and quality of life.

Ted brings his penetrating mind and wide experience to help every willing person be, do, and have more.

While it sounds incredulous to those stuck in yesterday's struggle mindset, you can cause a quantum leap in your income and profits, while working less - a lot less - and dramatically up both your personal satisfaction in life and your contributions to the world at the same time.

An author, a sales & marketing ace, a former professor of business communications at California State University, minister-at-large Ted Ciuba reminds us a quantum leap is a phenomenon of Nature in which one makes explosive, permanent performance and profit gains without passing through all the incremental steps in-between.

For years he's been teaching, training, and coaching ordinary people to access their extraordinary powers of achievement.

They call it *holomagic*.

Tune into his message, you'll be better off for it.

Find out more at http://ThinkRich.com

"Who Else Wants Quantum Coach and Author Ted Ciuba To Stimulate A Quantum Leap In Your Group?"

Schedule permitting, Dr. Ted Ciuba welcomes keynote, speaking and training invitations from businesses, churches, organizations, associations, & promoters.

Combines the spiritual purpose of quantum consciousness as per *The John Gospel Code* with the quantum performance message of *The New Think And Grow Rich, 101 Quantum Success Secrets,* and *Sub 4 Minute Extra Mile.*

For anyone in wholesome pursuit of money, a career, sales, indeed, achievement of any kind, as well as a life and service.

Through a brief, relevant pre-event questionnaire, presentation is made unique to each group.

To start conversation:

www.ThinkRich.com/invite

+1-615-662-3169

Ted Ciuba On Stage In LA

Defy & Re-Define The Status Quo In Short, Regular, Focused, Intense, Intended Training Sessions

www.BigBriefMoments.com

Complete your collection! Give a meaningful gift!

The *Sub 4 Minute Extra Mile* Series

High impact training focused on human potential, clear goals, marketing, & that holomagic c^2 factor

To get ahead you've got to go the *extra mile*

Redefine personal & professional possibility!

A sampling of what you'll find…

Vol: Title

001: Create Your Life By Design

002: Know Your Purpose, Embrace Adventure

003: That HoloMagic c2 Factor

004: A Single Reason Why

005: Same Winds, Different Direction

And many more!

http://BigBriefMoments.com

www.BigBriefMoments.com

Quantum Leap Mind Training
Neural Repatterning System

"How Quickly Would Your Life Improve If You Began Using The Untapped 90% Of Your Brain To Bring You Excellence?"

Revolutionary neuroscience driven!

Uses amazing new *neurosynergist® sound technology!*

Stanford neuroscientist finds key to easy permanent change through "structural brain change"

Quantum Leap Mind Training

Quantum Leap Mind Training is the only deep mind wealth training program in the world

1) based on the proven principles of *The NEW Think And Grow Rich*

2) using the patented neurosynergist® sound technology.

Reprogram yourself with knowledge, skills, & attitudes of visionary practical achievers.

Put this powerful **neural repatterning system** to work for you!

www.QuantumLeapMindTraining.com

"Amazing New Audio Program Gives You Both The Magic Formula To Riches & Most Effective Technology To Make It Happen Quickly And Easily!"

Audio Version of…

The New Think and Grow Rich
Quantum Version

by Ted Ciuba

Read by the Author!

Get the full story at…

This goes way BEYOND the amazing material captured in the book, *The NEW Think and Grow* by Ted Ciuba, into...

Learning Styles

All the "content" in the world, put in book form just doesn't make the connection with most people...

It's just a fact, most people find reading too much a struggle to put up with...

Some people find it impossible to get the meaning from squiggles on a page...

"I read the book years and years ago, but I didn't get the depth of it till I heard you narrating it."

Vita Buffa

www.TheNewThinkAndGrowRichAudio.com

101 Quantum Success Secrets

Author Ted Ciuba put these quantum secrets together and makes them freely available to you. **$197 value, *FREE!***

101 Success Secrets
101 Training Sessions
101 Seconds Each

Turn your life around.
  Stay focused.
    Achieve your dreams.

www.ThinkRich.com/101successsecrets

 Think Rich Ministries

Donate To Think Rich Ministries

It does take money to spread the Word throughout this material world. All donations are appreciated and are invested to spread Quantum Humanism.

www.ThinkRich.com/donate

www.ThinkRichRadio.com

"Voice Of Quantum Humanism"

Relevant conversations for today.

"Discover The "Secret" In A Magical Mastermind Study Of The 1937 *Original Publication* Of Napoleon Hill's Success Classic, *Think And Grow Rich*!"

Achiever's MasterMind

Achiever's MasterMind
You actively participate in working study sessions...
Designed With The Sole Purpose Of Making You Wealthy!

www.AchieversMasterMind.com

Includes:

4. Sixteen Achiever's MasterMind Sessions In Audio
5. Achiever's MasterMind Study Chapters
6. *Achiever's MasterMind* Study Guides

Bonuses include word-for-word transcriptions!

- How to do direct imprinting into your nervous system, so that you're driven to success!

- How to harness the awesome unseen power that has created Fortunes with one secret 6-step technique. (Takes less than 5 minutes to implement.)

- The 8-part, no-fail secret the winners in the wealth game use to... Create your own "breaks"

- And much, much more!

www.AchieversMasterMind.com

East-West Success MasterMind
Merging The Success Secrets Of Two Worlds

"If You're Looking For That Decided Edge That Can Accelerate You To Riches!…"

Author of *The NEW Think And Grow Rich*, Ted Ciuba, journeyed East to forge this collaboration. The entire event was captured, & is available to you now as the…

East-West Success MasterMind
www.EastWestSuccessMasterMind.com

Share the excitement that got people tuning in from Singapore, Malaysia, China, Hong Kong, Vietnam, Korea, Philippines, Thailand, India, Australia, UK, USA, Africa, and Latin America!

The purpose of the MasterMind is quite simple...

In a MasterMind study of the success philosophy outlined in the original *Think And Grow Rich*…

> ➤ To merge the BEST of both East and West to enable any willing human being, anywhere on this planet *or any other planet or moon*, to THINK WITH INTENT…

> ➤ To control and direct your thinking to receive the *natural result* of RICHES in your life!

"One of the most important days of my life was the day I began to read Think and Grow Rich." - W. Clement Stone

"I was invited to participate in the MasterMind *study of* Think And Grow Rich *by my friend Ted Ciuba. That 8-week program transformed my own Consciousness of Wealth...* - Dan Klatt

www.EastWestSuccessMasterMind.com

Finally Discovered!
Bible Secrets Hidden 1,917 Years Laid Bare

The John Gospel CODE
Unveiling The ContRaBanD Message
by Ted Ciuba

To sum up John's problem and his charge…

➢ John is the only person on Earth
in possession of the illumined
words Jesus spoke to his
initiatic inner circle
that **fateful final evening**…

John wanted to effectively transmit
the **mystic message** of Jesus to a
future epoch of humanity through a
present **age of mistrust and
intrigue**…

He did what he was inspired to do.
He coded it into his mysterious story
about the Christ, which became the
anchor gospel of the Biblical canon,
awaiting the magic day it could
breathe again.

The *Original* Message Unveiled!

Today we find ourselves with the code – given us in recent
years by quantum physics – which allows us to unveil the
contraband message John coded into his unundersatandable but
politically correct words.

It tells a different, far more glorious story than you've been led
to believe.

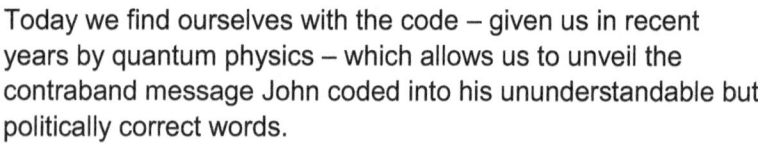

www.TheJohnGospelCode.com

➢ In bluntest contradiction to the mis-guided thesis the Bible condemns psychic skills…

"The Bible promises psychic sensitivities as a natural concomitant to the spiritual life!"

Samuel is psychic, David keeps Gad on retainer as a psychic, Ezekiel is psychic, Peter is psychic.

The Bible, *Genesis* through *Revelation*, is **revealed through channeling**, after all.

Book reveals the **psychic dimension** is the very channel established and used by God to communicate with humanity.

➢ The stories of the Bible speak with mythic significance

The boundaries of the material world do not confine Spirit and Soul

➢ The setting is the ancient Middle East,
    The location is everywhere; the time is always

Psi and its marvels interest everyone…

➢ On the other hand, **psi ability** calls its own…
➢ Some special individuals among us are awakening now

Psychic And Paranormal Phenomena In The Bible leads you in **develop**ing **your own psychic sensitivities** today.

Recommended Business Resources

ThinkRich.com/business

www.AutoPilotRiches.com

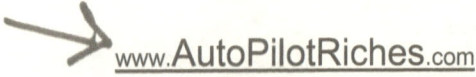

The net's premier **integrated ecommerce solution**.

Includes unlimited products, unlimited database, unlimited autoresponders. Compatible with all merchant accounts, PayPal, etc

 www.FastCashDomains.com

The net's leading domain supplier. Easy management.

 www.GatorWebsiteHosting.com

Unlimited Web Hosting! Unlimited disk space. Unlimited bandwidth! Easy, Affordable.

24/7/365 technical support

How To Get Rich On The Internet

www.HowToGetRichOnTheInternet.com

Mail Order In The Internet Age

www.MailOrderInTheInternetAge.com